Contents

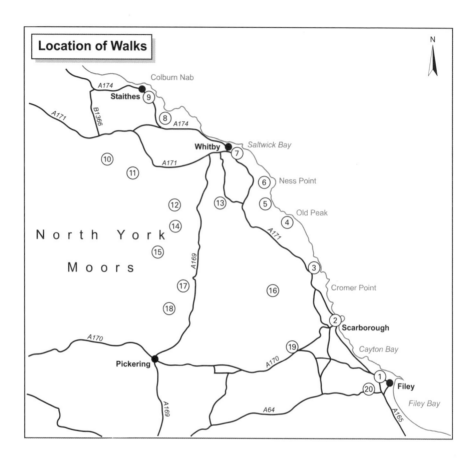

Location of Walks

Holiday Walks
in
North Yorkshire

Brian Conduit

Published by Sigma Leisure – an imprint of
Sigma Press, Stobart House, Pontyclerc, Penybanc Road
Ammanford, Carmarthenshire SA18 3HP

British Library Cataloguing in Publication Data

A CIP record for this book is available from the British Library

ISBN: 978-1-85058-867-2

Typesetting and Design by: Sigma Press, Ammanford, Wales

Maps: © Bute Cartographics

Photographs: © Brian Conduit

Cover photographs:
Main picture: Whitby Abbey
Left, from top downwards: Steam train at Grosmont station, Cayton Bay, Bridge over the River Esk at Lealholm, looking across the River Esk to Whitby

Printed by: Bell & Bain Limited, Glasgow

Disclaimer: The information in this book is given in good faith and is believed to be correct at the time of publication. Care should always be taken when walking in hill country. Where appropriate, attention has been drawn to matters of safety. The author and publisher cannot take responsibility for any accidents or injury incurred whilst following these walks. Only you can judge your own fitness, competence and experience. Do not rely solely on sketch maps for navigation: we strongly recommend the use of appropriate Ordnance Survey (or equivalent) maps.

Introduction to
the North Yorkshire Coast

With its glorious sandy beaches and spectacular scenery, the North Yorkshire coast has long been a favourite holiday destination. As early as the middle years of the 17th century Scarborough began to develop as a spa when wealthy visitors came to take the waters, believing that they could cure all sorts of ailments. In the 18th century sea bathing for the first time was considered to bestow healthy benefits on its practitioners and Scarborough, along with other towns around Britain's coastline, became a fashionable resort, rivalling the attractions of the popular inland spas.

At first the visitors were members of the aristocracy but in the 19th and early 20th centuries two main national developments caused seaside resorts throughout Britain, including Scarborough and the neighbouring coastal towns of Filey and Whitby, to expand rapidly. These were improvements in transport and an increase in leisure time for working people.

From the 1830s onwards all three resorts became linked with the main rail network and with each other. This enabled middle and working class visitors, especially industrial workers seeking an escape from the noise and grime of Victorian Leeds, Bradford and Sheffield, to reach the Yorkshire coast for the first time. Unlike many other holiday areas, the Yorkshire resorts have retained their rail links, although the line between Whitby and Scarborough became a victim of the 'Beeching Axe' in the 1960s. Even this has proved to be something of a mixed blessing as the line was subsequently converted into a bridleway for horse riders, cyclists and walkers. The Beeching Axe itself was an indication that railways were becoming less important than road transport, a development that began in the inter-war years with the growth of coach travel and accelerated from the 1950s and 1960s onwards with the advent of mass car ownership.

Easy and cheap transport by itself would not have revolutionised the growth of resorts in this country without the increase in leisure. From the late 19th century onwards the number of bank holidays per year grew and more and more people were able to take holiday breaks at the seaside. Particularly significant was the Holidays with Pay Act of 1938 by which, for the first time, all workers in Britain were entitled to a weeks' paid holiday.

The heyday of the North Yorkshire coast as a holiday destination was the first half of the 20th century, reaching a peak in the 1950s and 1960s when thousands flocked to its beaches. This was the era when many people had the time and money to go on holiday but still went mainly to British seaside resorts because the cheap package holiday to sunnier and warmer climates was yet to become a serious competitor. This competition began on a large scale in the 1970s but despite this, the Yorkshire coast has retained much of its appeal and popularity.

It is not hard to see why. Apart from the beaches – some of the finest in the country – a major attraction is the spectacular coastline. The whole length of the coast from just north of Scarborough almost to the mouth of the Tees – except for a small area around Whitby – is part of the North York Moors National Park and a continuous coastal footpath, part of the Cleveland Way, runs along the coast from Filey to Saltburn-by-the-Sea. As well as the coast, there is superb walking inland across open moorland and through secluded valleys, through attractive villages and areas of forest, in the national park and further south on the edge of the Yorkshire Wolds. Interesting old country pubs and cosy village tea rooms only add to the pleasures of walking in this area.

So if you want a change from relaxing on the beach, strolling along the pier or making sand castles, go for a walk either along the coast or inland. You will get fresh air and exercise, enjoy superb scenery and appreciate even more that well-earned ice cream, fish and chips, cup of tea, pint of beer or three course meal afterwards. And you do not necessarily have to wait for good weather as even on a bad day, you can still enjoy a walk as long as you are adequately dressed and shod.

The Walks

The 20 walks range from 2½ to 6½ miles (4km to 10.5km) in length and are all well within the capabilities of most people. As well as varying in length, they vary in difficulty and the nature of the terrain and some are inevitably more strenuous and involve more hill climbing than others.

Read carefully the introductory information at the start of each walk in order to decide what suits you best. The majority of the routes are accessible by public transport from the nearest resort and information on buses and trains is provided. Three linear walks have been included where you can leave the car at the end of the walk, travel by bus or train to the starting point and walk back to your car. On such walks it is generally better to use the public transport first so that you can relax and take your time on the walk and not have to rush in order to catch a particular bus or train, especially where these are infrequent.

Maps
Explorer maps are the best for walkers. The vast majority of walks in this guide are covered by Ordnance Survey Explorer map OL27 (North York Moors – Eastern area) and just three are covered by Explorer 301 (Scarborough, Bridlington & Flamborough Head). It is always advisable to take the relevant map with you as the sketch maps in this book are only a rough guide.

Public transport
For information about bus and train services and timetables contact Traveline either by visiting www.traveline.org.uk or phoning 0871 200 2233. Alternatively contact the local tourist information centre.

Tourist Information Centres
The tourist information centres at Scarborough, Whitby and Filey have the same telephone number (01723 383636) and email address (tourismbureau@scarborough.gov.uk).

There is also The Moors National Park Centre near Danby; tel: 01439 772737, email: moorscentre@northyorkmoors-npa.gov.uk

Walk 1. Cayton Bay to Filey

Introduction

At the start there is a superb view looking across Cayton Bay to Scarborough and its imposing cliff top castle. Towards the end come equally spectacular views over Filey Bay to the distant chalk cliffs of Flamborough Head. In between you walk along a relatively undemanding stretch of the Cleveland Way, enjoying some fine cliff scenery.

Distance	5½ miles/8.9km
Start	Cayton Bay, near the junction of the A165 and the road to Cayton by the entrance to Cayton Bay Holiday Village, grid ref TA066843. From the bus station at Filey take East Yorkshire bus 121 and get off at Cayton Bay Holiday Village
Finish	Filey, corner of The Crescent and Belle Vue Street, grid ref TA120806
Parking	Car parks at Filey
Getting there by car	Filey is 7miles south of Scarborough, take the A165 and then the A1039
Public transport	East Yorkshire bus 121 from Scarborough, Northern Rail trains from Scarborough
Terrain	Almost entirely along a gently undulating stretch of the coast path
Refreshments	Pubs, cafés and fish and chip shops at Filey
Map	OS Explorer 301

The Walk

1. **Start by walking towards the traffic island on the A165 but before reaching it, bear right down a tarmac drive which passes under the main road to a T-junction. Turn right and at a public footpath sign, turn left along a tarmac track towards the sea.**

Ahead of you are the flat, golden sands of Cayton Bay and to the left is a magnificent view looking towards the headland on which stands the ruins of Scarborough Castle. The beach at Cayton Bay has been popular with generations of holidaymakers to this part of the Yorkshire coast, hence the large number of caravan sites and holiday parks in the vicinity, and in more recent years it has become something of a surfing centre.

2. **Where the track bears right, you also bear right onto a parallel grassy path, here joining the Cleveland Way which you follow to**

Cayton Bay

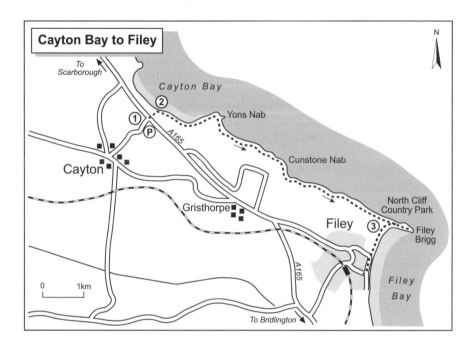

Filey, a distance of 5 miles (8km) according to the signpost. The coast path is easy to follow and this stretch of it is relatively undemanding. Keep on the grassy cliff top all the while, following the regular Cleveland Way signs and passing to the left of two large holiday parks. Later Filey and its bay come into view. After about 3 miles (4.8km), you reach the neck of the narrow promontory of Filey Brigg where there is a fingerpost. Bear right to a stone monument that marks the start of both the Cleveland Way and Wolds Way and keep ahead to a sandy track.

3. Bear right along it to North Bay Country Park on the edge of Filey. Keep to the left of the car park along the cliff top and in the far corner descend a long flight of steps into a wooded ravine. Cross the road at the bottom, ascend an almost equally long flight of steps on the other side and continue along the cliff top. To the right the sturdy tower of Filey's medieval church can be seen. At the end of the cliff descend another flight of steps that twist and turn through the trees down to a road and turn left. Follow the road as it bends right above the beach and take the first road on the right (Carrgate

Hill). Head uphill and when you see a flight of steps on the left, climb them to emerge onto a road near the corner of Belle Vue Street and The Crescent, the finishing point of the walk.

Filey is a smaller, quieter and more sedate version of Scarborough. It is well endowed with parks, gardens and green open spaces, has a superb sandy beach and retains a pleasantly old fashioned air. For centuries it was a small fishing and farming village until the 18th century when it began to emerge as a coastal resort. Two events in the 19th century accelerated that growth: the coming of the railway in 1846-47and the building of The Crescent, a row of large and elegant Victorian buildings overlooking the sea. This was the work of John Wilkes Unett, an enterprising Birmingham solicitor, and was completed in the 1850s.

The Crescent, Filey

Walk 2. Historic Scarborough

Introduction

This walk introduces you to many of Scarborough's most interesting and attractive features and illustrates the various aspects of the town's long history. It starts at the colourful and lively harbour, where most of the traditional features of the British seaside are to be found – ice cream parlours, fish and chip shops, amusement arcades – and takes you along South Bay to the Spa Complex, the origins of Scarborough's development as a holiday resort. After a climb up to the cliff top, where there is a choice between steps and the cliff railway, you walk past elegant Victorian terraces and on through the main shopping centre. A climb up some of the narrow streets of Old Scarborough brings you to the Norman castle and medieval church and fine views over North Bay. Then comes a final descent to Marine Drive which you follow below the castle headland to return to the start.

The Harbour at Scarborough

Distance	4½ miles/7.2km
Start	Scarborough, by the harbour, grid ref TA048887
Parking	Plenty of car parks in Scarborough
Getting there by car	A number of main roads – A165, A170, A171 and A64 – lead to Scarborough which is 7 miles north of Filey and 20 miles south of Whitby
Public transport	East Yorkshire bus 121 from Filey and Arriva bus 93 and X93 from Whitby; Northern Rail trains from Filey, Hull, York and Leeds
Terrain	Mainly easy town walking on pavements and tarmac paths, 2 climbs
Refreshments	Plenty of choice of restaurants, pubs, coffee shops and fish and chip shops at Scarborough
Map	OS Explorer 301 or pick up a town map from the Tourist Information Centre

The Walk

Scarborough, the largest resort on the North Yorkshire coast, claims to be the first holiday resort in the country. Originally founded by the Vikings, it remained a small fishing harbour huddled around the base of its castle until the late 17th century when a small stream flowing into South Bay was found to have health-giving properties. As a result Scarborough became a spa and its popularity increased in the 18th century when it became a fashionable place for aristocratic visitors to come and take the waters. As early as 1735 there was the first recorded use of a bathing machine here. A major development was the coming of the railways in the 1840s which linked Scarborough with the great industrial towns and cities of Yorkshire. Thousands of middle and working class holidaymakers flocked to enjoy its many delights,

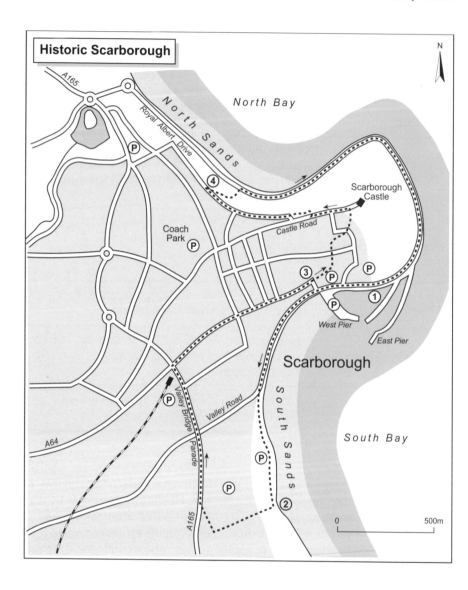

principally the two fine and extensive sandy beaches either side of the bold headland on which stand the ruins of the Norman castle. These assets, enhanced by other amenities – parks, gardens and an annual cricket festival – have ensured its continued popularity.

1. **Facing the sea, turn right along the road beside the harbour and continue along a tarmac path beside South Sands. Pass below the huge Grand Hotel and continue to the Spa Complex.**

The imposing Grand Hotel, a fine example of Victorian architecture, dominates the skyline of South Bay. It was built in the 1860s and was one of the first purpose built hotels in Europe. It was also one of the largest with 365 bedrooms, one for every day of the year.

The spa buildings have had a chequered history. Since the first spa was built in the middle of the 18th century, it has been frequently damaged either by storms or fire and rebuilt several times. The present buildings date from a major rebuilding in 1880 and comprise the Grand Hall plus theatre, lounges and sun court, with cafés and bars.

In their various ways the Grand Hotel, Spa Complex and Prince of Wales Terrace – the latter to be walked along shortly – all illustrate Scarborough's heyday as a popular and fashionable resort.

Looking across South Bay to Scarborough Castle

2. From the Spa, either turn right up any of the steep, zigzag paths to the Esplanade or – if you wish to conserve your energy for the later climb up to the castle – take the Cliff Railway. At the top, cross the road and keep ahead along the elegant Prince of Wales Terrace, bordered by gardens on the left. Turn right into West Street and in front of a church, turn right downhill along Ramshill Road and cross Valley Bridge into the town centre. By the railways station turn right along Westborough and continue downhill along first Newborough and later Eastborough.

3. At the bottom of the hill where the road curves right down to the harbour, turn left up an alley into Old Scarborough. After following it around a left bend, turn right along Princess Street, lined by attractive old houses. At a T-junction turn left steeply uphill and just after a left bend, turn right up a flight of steps to the castle. Keep ahead to the entrance if visiting the castle but at the top of the steps the walk continues to the left along a tarmac path.

Prehistoric settlements and a Roman signal station occupied the headland before the castle was built by a Norman baron, William le Gros, in 1136. It was soon seized by Henry II who built the keep in the 1150s, the castle's most striking remaining feature. It was an important royal stronghold on the east coast, especially significant during the Scottish Wars, and like most medieval castles it saw action in the Civil War when it was twice besieged. Also like most castles it was destroyed on Cromwell's orders after that conflict, a process

Norman keep of Scarborough Castle

hastened by the action of the weather on its exposed cliff top location. However this was not the end of its military history because both the castle and town were surprisingly bombarded by German warships at the start of World War I in 1914, an event that resulted in 19 deaths.

On emerging onto a road, keep ahead passing to the right of St Mary's church.

The church dates mainly from the late 12th century with later additions. It was badly damaged in the 1640s during the Civil War sieges of the nearby castle when both the chancel and tower were destroyed. This is why it is much shorter than before. The tower was rebuilt around 1670 and there was a further restoration in the Victorian period.

Many people come to visit the tomb of Anne Bronte, one of the famous trio of literary sisters and the only member of the family not to be buried at Haworth. She had fallen seriously ill early in 1849 but thought that a trip to Scarborough would do her good. This was not to be and she died while here at the age of 29. Her sister Charlotte, who had accompanied her, took the decision to have her buried at Scarborough rather than take the body back to Haworth, not an easy journey in those days.

Opposite the church turn right into Mulgrave Place and turn left along a path above North Bay. The path later widens out and continues beside Queens Parade.

4. **Turn sharp right downhill along Albert Road which bends left and continues down to Marine Drive. Turn sharp right and follow the road as it curves right below Castle Hill to return to the harbour.**

Walk 3. Cloughton and Hayburn Wyke

Introduction

The first part of the route is along the track of a former railway. Then follows a descent through woodland to the waterfall and stony beach at Hayburn Wyke, after which you climb steeply through more woodland to emerge onto the open cliff top. The final leg is an attractive walk along the coast path to Cloughton Wyke, enjoying dramatic views ahead of Scarborough Castle on its headland. From here a quiet lane leads back to the start.

Distance	4½ miles/7.2km
Start	Cloughton, road junction at the north end of the village, grid ref TA010947
Parking	Roadside parking at Cloughton
Getting there by car	Cloughton is on the A171 5 miles north of Scarborough and 15 miles south of Whitby
Public transport	Arriva bus 93 and X93 from Scarborough and Whitby, Scarborough and District bus 15 from Scarborough
Terrain	Mixture of flat walking along a disused railway track followed by an undulating stretch of the coast path
Refreshments	Pubs at Cloughton, tea room at the former Cloughton station, pub at Hayburn Wyke
Map	OS Explorer OL27

Looking down on Hayburn Wyke from Coast Path

The Walk

1. **Begin by turning down Newlands Lane. In front of the bridge over a disused railway track, bear left onto a path, descend steps to the track and turn left along it.**

   This is the track of the former Whitby to Scarborough Railway which opened in 1885 and closed down in 1965. During its 80 year history, it carried thousands of passengers along this exceptionally attractive 20 mile stretch of the Yorkshire coast. Fortunately it has been put to good use as almost the whole length was converted into a bridleway for horse riders, cyclists and walkers.

2. **After 1½ miles (2.4km) and immediately after passing through a gate, turn right along a tarmac track, signposted to Hayburn Wyke, passing the Hayburn Wyke Inn and continuing on to a stile. Climb it, keep ahead and at a yellow-waymarked post, turn right and head**

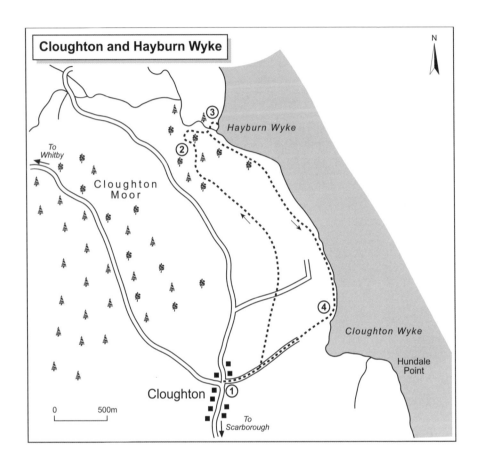

downhill. Climb another stile, here entering the National Trust property of Hayburn Wyke, and descend through woodland. At a junction of paths turn left, continue down, via steps in places, and look out for a waymarked post. The main route turns right here along the Cleveland Way but keep ahead down more steps for a short detour to the stony beach at Hayburn Wyke.

The proximity of the railway meant that from Victorian times up to the closure of the line in 1965, Hayburn Wyke was more accessible and more visited than now and was a favourite location for picnics. It certainly is a beautiful spot with splendid cliff scenery and Hayburn

Beck cascading over huge rocks onto the stony beach. 'Wyke' is a Scandinavian word meaning narrow inlet.

3. **Return to the waymarked post and turn left onto a slabbed path for a long and steady climb through woodland, looking out for the regular Cleveland Way signs. At the top you emerge from the trees and continue along the cliff top, initially by a left field edge and later along an enclosed path. As the path starts to descend, grand views open up ahead of Scarborough, with the castle dominating the scene. At a fingerpost by a wooden bench, keep ahead, still on the Cleveland Way, descending more steeply and continuing down steps through woodland. After leaving the trees, keep ahead along an undulating path to Cloughton Wyke, another attractive inlet.**

4. **At a fork, take the right hand path, here leaving the Cleveland Way, and head up steps to a bench at the end of a lane and a small parking area. Walk along the lane back to Cloughton.**

Waterfall at Hayburn Wyke

Walk 4. Ravenscar

Introduction

The first part of the walk is along a flat stretch of the Cleveland Way, with fine views across Robin Hood's Bay and impressive cliff scenery. After a short section along a lane, the return leg to Ravenscar is along the track of the former Whitby to Scarborough Railway.

Distance	3½ miles/5.6km
Start	Ravenscar, corner of Raven Hall Road and Station Road by the National Trust Coastal Centre, grid ref NZ980016
Parking	Free roadside parking area at the start
Getting there by car	Ravenscar is 11 miles north of Scarborough and 7 miles south of Whitby and is reached by side roads signposted from the A171
Public transport	Scarborough and District bus 115 from Scarborough
Terrain	Flat and easy stretch of coast path followed by a disused railway track
Refreshments	Hotel and tea room at Ravenscar
Map	OS Explorer OL27

The Walk

Ravenscar has been described as 'the town that never was'. Originally called Peak, it was renamed in the early 20th century when an ambitious scheme was launched to transform it into a major coastal resort to rival nearby Scarborough. Houses and roads were built and sewers were laid but only a few houses were taken. Although the location was attractive enough and the railway line between Scarborough and Whitby had broken down its previous isolation, some serious disadvantages had been

The broad sweep of Robin Hood's Bay from Ravenscar

overlooked. Apart from its exposed location, the main problems were that the local beaches were rocky and it was a long and quite difficult walk to get to them. The plans were abandoned and in 1913 the building company was wound up. Today Ravenscar remains a small but attractive backwater, popular with walkers using the Cleveland Way.

Before the plans to turn Ravenscar into a holiday resort, the area had been a major centre for the extraction of alum and the remains of some of the alum quarries can be seen just to the north of the village. The National Trust Coastal Centre at the start of the walk has information and displays on the history of the area, particularly concentrating on its geological and industrial heritage.

1. **Facing the entrance to the Raven Hall Hotel, turn right along Station Road. At a Cleveland Way sign to Scarborough, turn left along a broad track and on reaching the top of the cliffs, turn right. Now**

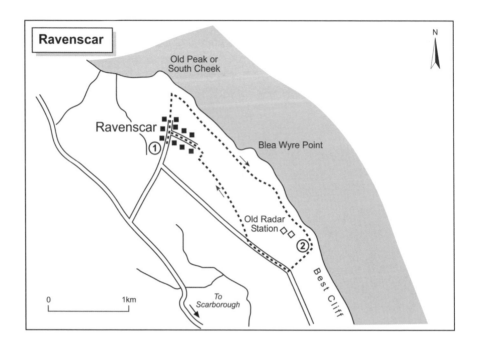

follows a stretch of easy and relatively flat cliff top walking, with grand views along the coast, especially looking northwards across the broad expanse of Robin Hood's Bay.

After about 1¼ miles (2km), you pass the remains of Ravenscar Radar Station. This was one of a chain built in 1940 around Britain's coastline to detect the approach of German ships and aircraft during the Second World War. In front of it is a Coastguard look-out, built slightly earlier in 1935 and also used in the war.

2. Shortly after passing the look-out, turn right over a stile at a footpath sign, walk along the right edge of a field and go through a gate onto a narrow lane. Turn right and just after crossing a disused railway bridge, turn right over a stile and descend steps to the track of the former Whitby to Scarborough Railway. Turn left and follow it back to the remains of the station buildings at Ravenscar. After climbing a stile, keep ahead along a tarmac track, one of the platforms of the former station.

The station at Ravenscar had the distinction of being the highest point on the Whitby to Scarborough Railway, 631 feet (192m) above sea level.

From the platform turn right, descend steps and walk across a parking area to a road. Turn left for the short distance back to the start.

A stile gives access to the remains of a World War II radar station near Ravenscar

Walk 5. Robin Hood's Bay and Boggle Hole

Introduction

The first part of the walk is a pleasant and easy stroll along the track of the former Whitby to Scarborough railway. A short stretch along a lane to the steep-sided inlet of Boggle Hole brings you to the coast path and from here you climb via a flight of steps onto the cliff top. This is followed by a most attractive walk along the cliffs to Robin Hood's Bay, with superb views over the bay and fishing village. After descending into the village, the final stretch is a steep climb up the main street back to the start.

Distance	4 miles/6.4km
Start	Robin Hood's Bay, Bank Top car park, grid ref NZ952052
Parking	Bank Top car park at Robin Hood's Bay, or if full use the larger Station car park ¼ mile (400m) to the north
Getting there by car	Robin Hood's Bay is situated on the B1447 15 miles north of Scarborough and 5 miles south of Whitby and is signposted from the A171
Public transport	Arriva buses 93 and X93 from Scarborough and Whitby
Terrain	Flat walking along a former railway track and lane followed by a climb via steps onto the coast path, fairly steep climb at the end
Refreshments	Pubs and cafés at Robin Hood's Bay
Map	OS Explorer OL27

The picturesque jumble of houses and cottages at Robin Hood's Bay cling to the side of the cliffs

The Walk

1. Turn left out of the car park and take the first road on the left (Thorpe Lane). At a Cycleway sign where the road curves right, turn left onto a tarmac track, part of the former railway line between Whitby and Scarborough which closed down in 1965.

    If starting from Station car park, walk in front of the former station buildings, continue down a path to Thorpe Lane and turn right to reach the Cycleway sign.

    Keep along this track for 1½ miles (2.4km) as far as a fork where you take the left hand track and descend a flight of steps to a lane. Turn left, follow the lane to Boggle Hole car park and keep ahead, later descending along the side of a ravine to the small and secluded bay at Boggle Hole.

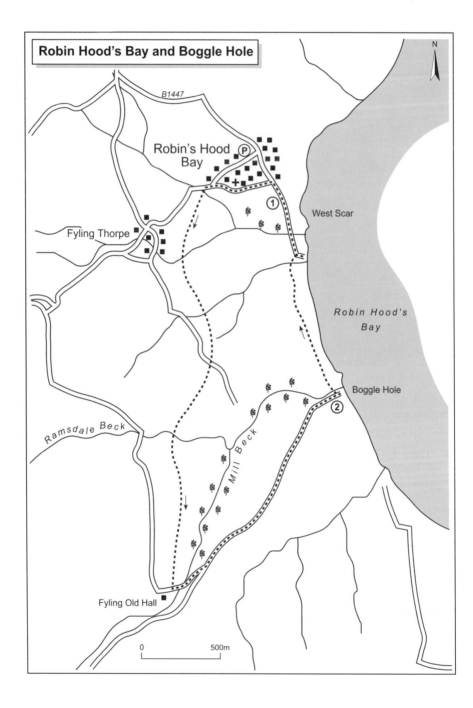

Robin Hood's Bay and Boggle Hole

B1447

Robin's Hood Bay

P

West Scar

Fyling Thorpe

①

Robin Hood's Bay

Boggle Hole

②

Ramsdale Beck

Mill Beck

Fyling Old Hall

N

0   500m

Boggle Hole is a deep crevice in the coastline just to the south of Robin Hood's Bay and is particularly popular with fossil hunters. The impressive former mill building has been converted into a youth hostel.

2. **A few yards beyond a Cleveland Way sign on the right, turn sharp left down steps and at the bottom turn right to cross a footbridge over the beck. On the other side of the footbridge ascend a long flight of steps and continue along the coast path to a gate. Go through and for the rest of the route you enjoy superb views of the picturesque huddle of buildings that make up Robin Hood's Bay. After the next gate, turn right and the path bends left and continues towards the village, descending a long flight of steps to a T-junction. Turn left, go down more steps and walk along an alley to a T-junction in the village centre.**

Many would rate Robin Hood's Bay as the most picturesque place on the Yorkshire coast. Its jumble of old cottages, houses and pubs

Splendid Coastal Scenery near Robin Hood's Bay

cascade down the hillside to the beach at the bottom in a seemingly random fashion. Narrow streets and alleys lead off in all directions and houses seem to have been squeezed into impossible spaces. A wander around is a most pleasant experience, made better by the lack of cars which have to park at the top of the hill. In view of its previously almost inaccessible location, it is not surprising that in the 18th century Robin Hood's Bay was notorious for smuggling activities. Although it is a long way from Sherwood Forest and there is not a shred of evidence to link it with the legendary outlaw, it may have acquired its name from an old tale that Robin Hood once escaped from his pursuers by boarding a boat here.

At the T-junction turn left up Main Street and continue steeply uphill to return to the car parks.

Walk 6. Hawkser to Robin Hood's Bay

Introduction

After a brief stretch along a former railway track, the route heads downhill across fields to join the Cleveland Way. The rest of the walk is along this path as it follows a winding course around all the indentations of this stretch of the North Yorkshire coast and takes you through some outstanding and dramatic cliff scenery. Near the end come fine views across Robin Hood's Bay to the headland at Ravenscar.

Distance	4½ miles/7.2km
Start	Hawkser, by the Hare and Hounds pub, grid ref NZ925077. From the corner of Station Road and Thorpe Lane at Robin Hood's Bay, take Arriva bus 93/X93 to Hawkser and get off at the Hare and Hounds
Finish	Robin Hood's Bay, Station car park, grid ref NZ952055
Parking	Station and Bank Top car parks at Robin Hood's Bay
Getting there by car	Robin Hood's Bay is situated on the B1447 15 miles north of Scarborough and 5 miles south of Whitby and is signposted from the A171
Public transport	Arriva buses 93 and X93 from Scarborough and Whitby
Terrain	Former railway track and easy stretch of the coast path
Refreshments	Pub at Hawkser, pubs and cafés at Robin Hood's Bay
Map	OS Explorer OL27

The spectacular stretch of coast to the north of Robin Hood's Bay

The Walk

The pleasant village of Hawkser lies slightly inland from the coast and has a number of attractive old cottages. Whitby is only 3 miles to the north and the remains of its cliff top abbey can be seen from the village.

1. **Start by walking back along the village street, passing to the left of the pub. Follow the road as it curves left in the Robin Hood's Bay and Fylingthorpe direction – take care as at times there is no footway – and where the road bends right, keep ahead along the tarmac drive (Bottoms Lane) to Seaview and Northcliffe Holiday Parks. At a crossways turn right onto a rough track, once part of the former Whitby to Scarborough Railway.**

    For details of the Whitby to Scarborough Railway see Walk 3.

    Go through a gate, keep ahead and after ½ mile (800m) – just after passing a notice denoting an important wildlife site – look out for

a path on the left that leads to a stile by a National Trust sign for Bottom House. After climbing the stile, walk gently downhill along the left edge of a field towards the sea. Climb another stile, continue more steeply downhill, follow the field edge as it bends first to the left and then to the right and continue down to a stile.

2. Climb it, turn right onto the Cleveland Way and follow it to Robin Hood's Bay. The path is easy to follow as it keeps along the top of the cliffs all the way. At one point, after going through a kissing gate, you descend into a valley and go through another kissing gate. Eventually Robin Hood's Bay comes into view and shortly afterwards, go through a kissing gate and keep along the left edge of a field. Follow the edge to the left, go through a kissing gate, follow a path to the right, go through a gate and keep ahead along an enclosed path. After going through another gate, continue along

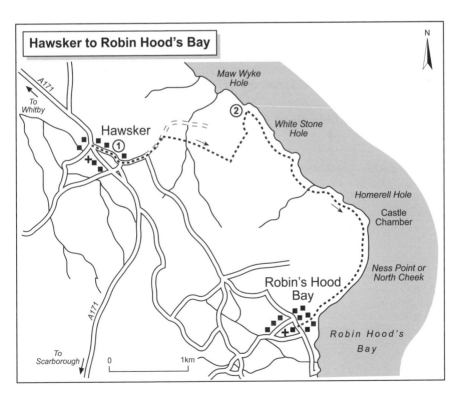

Coast to the north of Robin Hood's Bay

a road into Robin Hood's Bay to a road junction. The Station car park is just ahead.

For details of Robin Hood's Bay see Walk 5.

Walk 7. Whitby and Saltwick Nab

Introduction

A gentle walk across fields and along lanes on the edge of Whitby brings you to the coast path. You then follow an easy but at the same time dramatic stretch of the path, over Saltwick Nab and along the cliffs, enjoying fine views all the way, with the ruins of the cliff top abbey standing out prominently. From the abbey you descend the famous 199 steps that lead down past the church and through the old picturesque part of the town back to the start. One advantage of doing this walk in the recommended anti-clockwise direction is that the descent of these steps is a lot easier than the ascent.

Distance	3 miles/4.8km
Start	Whitby, Swing Bridge over the River Esk, grid ref NZ899111
Parking	Car parks at Whitby
Getting there by car	Whitby is situated just off the A171 20 miles north of Scarborough
Public transport	Arriva buses 93 and X93 from Scarborough; Northern Rail trains from Middlesbrough
Terrain	Quiet lanes and easy paths and tracks
Refreshments	Plenty of cafés, restaurants, pubs and fish and chip shops in Whitby
Map	OS Explorer OL27

The Walk

The sea is inseparable from Whitby and for much of its history this fishing port was largely cut off from the rest of the country by the surrounding moors and was only easily accessible by boat. In the 7th century an Anglo-Saxon monastery was founded here which became one of the great

Whitby harbour

centres of Christianity in Northumbria. Two famous names associated with Whitby are Captain Cook, who learnt the art of seamanship while apprenticed here, and Bram Stoker, author of Dracula, who wrote his famous novel while on holiday in the town. During the 18th and 19th centuries, the quarrying of jet, a black gemstone used in jewellery and only found in the vicinity of Whitby, was a flourishing industry. Although its popularity has declined, tourists still like to browse around the many shops in the old part of the town which sell items made from Whitby Jet and the Jet Heritage Centre in the town is well worth a visit.

In the Victorian era railway links with Scarborough and the industrial towns of Teesside ended its previous remoteness and isolation and Whitby took on a new role as a tourist centre and holiday resort. Nowadays its quaint, narrow, twisting streets that lie at the bottom of the 199 steps that lead up to the church and abbey are thronged with visitors during the summer months.

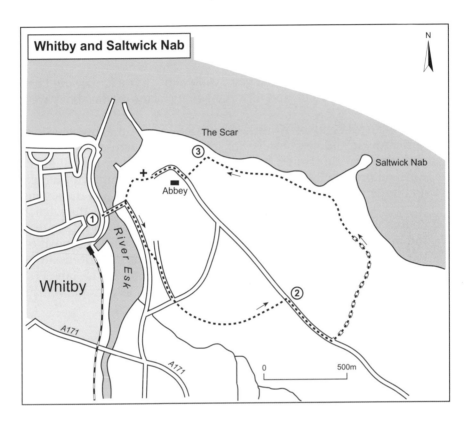

1. Facing downstream towards the sea, turn right and at a T-junction, turn right again. After about ¼ mile (400m), turn left up Boulby Bank and continue twisting and turning uphill to emerge onto a road (The Ropery). Keep ahead to a T-junction, cross over, walk up a tarmac drive and continue along an enclosed, slabbed path. The path joins a tarmac track. Continue along it and where this track ends at a farm, keep ahead through a kissing gate and walk along the right edge of a field to a lane.

2. Turn right and after ¼ mile (400m), turn left, at a public footpath sign, along the tarmac drive to Whitby Holiday Park. On reaching a Cleveland Way sign, turn left initially through the caravan park. Beyond the park, continue along the cliff top path over the promontory of Saltwick Nab and on towards Whitby. All the way

there are fine views ahead of the prominent landmark of Whitby
Abbey.

3. **After turning left through a gate, walk along a track, passing farm
    buildings on the right, and turn right along a lane by the abbey wall.**

The splendid ruins of Whitby Abbey stand high up above the town
and harbour and can be seen for miles around across much of the
surrounding countryside. It was originally founded by Oswy King of
Northumbria in 657and was a mixed monastic community of monks
and nuns, presided over by Abbess Hilda. In 664 it was the setting
for the famous synod which decided that the future of the English
church lay with the continental Roman Catholic church rather than
the more isolated Celtic church. Its easily visible cliff top position
made it an easy target for Viking raids and it was destroyed during
one of these in 867. Refounded by the Normans in the late 11th
century as a Benedictine abbey, it enjoyed a largely uneventful

The ruins of Whitby Abbey are a dominant feature for much of the walk

The impressive east end of Whitby Abbey

existence until its closure by Henry VIII and Thomas Cromwell in 1539. Despite subsequently falling into ruin, much of the impressive abbey church survives. This dates mainly from the 13th and 14th centuries and mostly remains to its full height.

Nearby is St Mary's church, a sturdy, fortress-looking structure. The church still retains some of its original 12th century work but has been enlarged and extensively restored over the centuries. It is especially noted for its rare unaltered 18th century interior.

The lane curves left and where it ends, turn right and descend the 199 steps, initially along the left edge of the churchyard, into the town. At the bottom continue along a cobbled street which bends left to rejoin the outward route and turn right to return to the bridge.

Looking across the entrance to Whitby harbour

8. Runswick Bay

Introduction

This is a 'there and back' walk along and above the superb sweep of Runswick Bay. The first part of the route, across the fine sandy beach, is followed by a climb along the side of a steep gully, ascending a long flight of steps to the cliff top. Then comes an exhilarating walk along one of the finest stretches of the Yorkshire coast to the prominent and dramatic headland of Kettle Ness. From here you retrace your steps to the start, enjoying spectacular views across the bay to Runswick village. Take your time and save this walk for a fine day in order to appreciate the views at their best. As it is a 'there and back' walk you can of course stop and retrace your steps whenever you feel like it.

Distance	3½ miles/5.6km
Start	Runswick Bay, Beach car park, grid ref NZ809160
Parking	Car parks at Runswick Bay
Getting there by car	Runswick Bay is 9 miles north of Whitby and is signposted from the A174
Public transport	Arriva buses 56 and X56 drop you at the top of the village
Terrain	Beach followed by cliff top walking, one lengthy climb and descent
Refreshments	Pubs and café at Runswick Bay
Map	OS Explorer OL27

The Walk

With its picturesque, white-painted cottages huddled against the side of a cliff, protected from the north winds and overlooking a glorious sandy beach, Runswick Bay has an idyllic situation. The original village was on a slightly different site but was destroyed by a major landslip in 1664. In the past this was an isolated and fairly inaccessible spot which made it an ideal location for smuggling. Although mostly a small fishing hamlet, some of the inhabitants of Runswick Bay later worked in the nearby alum quarries at Kettleness. Now it relies almost entirely on the holiday trade.

1. From the corner of the car park descend steps to the road and turn right downhill towards the sea. Follow the road around a right bend and bear right onto a path which keeps above the beach before descending to it. Continue across the sands, following the curve of the bay to the left.

The striking promontory of Kettle Ness

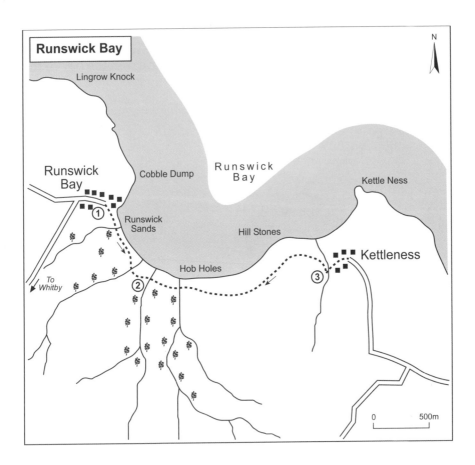

2. Just after passing some caves in the cliff face, turn right onto a rocky path through a narrow gully on the right side of a small beck. At an acorn symbol footpath post – this denotes that you are on the Cleveland Way – turn left to ford the beck. Now begins a long ascent up steps along the side of the gully, between trees and bushes in places, eventually emerging onto the cliff top. As you continue along the coast path, going through a series of gates, the views across the bay to the prominent headland of Kettle Ness are outstanding and to the right the tops of some of the spoil tips of the disused alum quarries can be seen. Shortly after descending into a dip and heading up again (via steps) you reach a track by a stile and Cleveland Way sign at Kettleness.

3. The Cleveland Way continues to the left but at this point retrace your steps back along the cliff top, down the steps and across the beach to the start, enjoying the superb views across the bay to the village and cliffs to the north.

Steps lead from the beach at Runswick Bay to the top of the cliff

Walk 9. Staithes and Port Mulgrave

Introduction

This is a walk of great scenic variety, embracing cliff tops, fields, woodland, distant moorland views and two contrasting villages. First you descend into the fascinating and highly atmospheric old fishing village of Staithes. A steep climb along the Cleveland Way brings you onto the cliffs for a bracing walk to the rather forgotten settlement of Port Mulgrave. Then comes a descent across fields and through woodland into the narrow valley of Dales Beck. After a climb out of the valley, followed by another descent to recross the beck, a final climb returns you to the start.

Distance	4 miles/6.4km
Start	Staithes, Bank Top car park, grid ref NZ781185
Parking	Car park at Staithes
Getting there by car	Staithes is situated just off the A174 10 miles north of Whitby
Public transport	Arriva buses 56 and X56 from Whitby to Staithes Lane, from there walk along the lane to the start
Terrain	Coast, field and woodland paths; three fairly energetic climbs
Refreshments	Pubs and cafés at Staithes, tea room (opening limited to Friday, Saturday and Sunday afternoons in summer) at Port Mulgrave
Map	OS Explorer OL27

The old fishing village of Staithes

The Walk

At the start the view is dominated by the huge Boulby Potash Mine, opened in 1973 and one of the deepest mines in Europe. It is a current reminder of the industrial heritage of this area; in Victorian times jet, alum and ironstone were mined locally, the latter serving the nearby industries of Teesside.

1. From the car park take the tarmac path signposted Footpath to Village and descend steps to the road. Turn right and head steeply downhill into Staithes. At the bottom, follow the cobbled street to

the right, continue past the Cod and Lobster pub and immediately turn right into Church Street.

The old village of Staithes occupies the eastern side of a deep and narrow inlet and its cottages seem to cling to the side of the cliff. As you descend the hill, it is like stepping back in time as, apart from being much quieter, Staithes seems to have changed little since Victorian times. Then it was a major fishing port as well being involved in the shipping of ore from nearby mines. Because of its unusual and dramatic location and highly picturesque appearance - it is a paradise for photographers - it later attracted a number of artists and now relies mainly on tourism. At the bottom of Church Street is Captain Cook's cottage: as a young man he was apprenticed

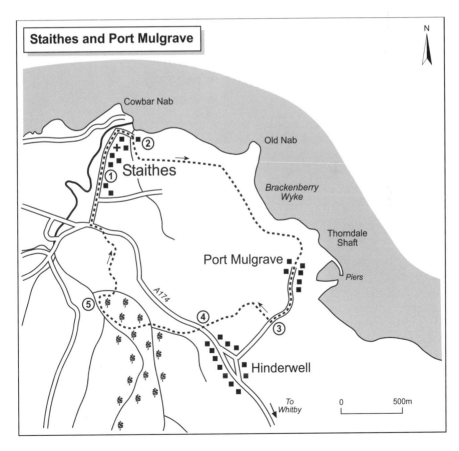

Staithes

here to a shop keeper before moving to Whitby and taking up seamanship.

2. Head steeply uphill and where the street ends by a public footpath sign 'Cleveland Way, Port Mulgrave', keep ahead up a slabbed path. At the next public footpath sign, turn left and continue up to emerge onto a tarmac track. Where the track ends, keep ahead along an enclosed path which widens into a track and continues to a gate. Go through, head up to another gate, go through that one and continue by a fence on the left. Where the fence bears left, keep ahead – still climbing – curving right by a fence on the left finally to emerge, via a gate, onto the cliff top. Keep ahead and shortly the houses of Port Mulgrave come into view. Follow the path as it turns right away from the coast, go through a gate and keep ahead along a track. The track becomes a tarmac lane which bends right into Port Mulgrave

   Although surrounded by superb coastal scenery, Port Mulgrave has a rather abandoned and forlorn air, comprising little more than a few Victorian terraces and a handful of modern properties perched on a cliff top above a deserted harbour. It is difficult to envisage it as a thriving centre of iron production and distribution in the 19th century.

3. Keep ahead along the lane for the tea room but at a public footpath sign by the end of a row of cottages, turn right along a track. Go through a gate, keep ahead briefly along a right field edge and at the next public footpath sign, follow the path to the left across fields to a stile in the field corner. After climbing it, head downhill along the left edge of a field and at a fence corner, keep ahead more steeply downhill to a stile. Climb it, continue down the left edge of the next field and pass beside a gate onto the A174. Cross over and turn right along a tarmac track.

4. At a public footpath sign, turn left down steps and walk along a path between bushes. The path curves left, descends quite steeply through woodland and eventually curves left again down to a beck. Cross a footbridge over it, keep ahead up to a fork and take the right hand path. Now comes the climb out of the valley as you head steeply uphill, via more steps, eventually emerging from the trees

at the top. Turn right along a grassy path which descends to a T-junction and turn right along a track. Head steeply downhill, curving first left and then right down to a footbridge over the beck.

5. Immediately turn right across an open area to the entrance to a caravan site and take the path to the left of it to a stile. Climb it and continue along a path lined by trees and bushes, curving left and heading up to a track at the top. Cross it, pass beside a redundant stile and go through a kissing gate. Continue along a fence-lined track, go through a kissing gate onto the A174 again and turn left. Take the first road on the right (Staithes Lane) to return to the start.

Coast between Staithes and Port Mulgrave

Walk 10. Danby Beacon

Introduction

From The Moors Centre, a steady climb along tracks, paths and a quiet lane brings you to the magnificent all-round viewpoint of Danby Beacon, 980 feet (299m) high. On the descent across open moorland and fields there are more grand and extensive views over upper Esk Dale to enjoy. This walk is best saved for a fine day and clear conditions in order to enjoy the superb views at their best.

Distance	4½ miles/7.2km
Start	The Moors National Park Centre near Danby, grid ref NZ716084
Parking	Car park at The Moors Centre
Getting there by car	The Moors Centre is about 13 miles to the east of Whitby, from the A169 take the winding road through Esk Dale via Grosmont, Egton Bridge, Glaisdale and Lealholm
Public transport	None
Terrain	Mainly moorland walking with one fairly steep climb and two gentler ones
Refreshments	Tea room at The Moors Centre
Map	OS Explorer OL27

The Walk

The Moors National Park Centre, located in a handsome former shooting lodge, occupies an idyllic position on the banks of the River Esk about ¾ mile (1.2km) from Danby village. There is all the information that you are likely to want to know here about the national park with an exhibition centre, gallery, shop, play areas and tea room. There are also plenty of books and leaflets about the many varied and excellent walks in the area.

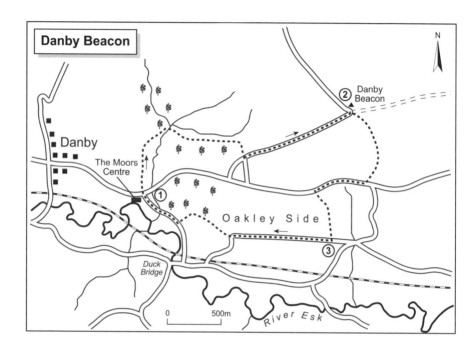

1. Turn right out of the car park, passing to the right of The Moors
   Centre, to a T-junction. Keep ahead through a gate, at a public
   footpath sign, and head gently uphill between trees by a wall on
   the right. Continue up to a gate, go through and keep ahead, by a
   wall on the left, to a waymarked gate. Do not go through it but turn
   right and head downhill along a path to a gate. Go through, continue
   gently downhill through trees and go through another gate. Where
   the path forks immediately ahead, take the right hand lower path
   and head down to a stile near the left field corner. Climb it, cross a
   footbridge over a beck and turn right alongside it. Look out for
   where you turn left to cross a duckboard over a patch of boggy
   ground, head across to a wall and turn left to head steeply uphill
   beside it. At one point you have to pick your way between
   boulders, after which the way continues more gently up. Follow the
   wall around a right bend to emerge onto a lane. Turn sharply left
   and head gently uphill for 1 mile (1.6km) to Danby Beacon.

   The present Danby Beacon, a striking example of modern design, was
   completed in 2008 and manages to combine a traditional appearance

with contemporary lines. It occupies an ancient site that over the centuries has served a number of purposes: Bronze Age burial mound, warning beacon since at least the time of the Napoleonic Wars and Second World War radar station. At a height of 980 feet (299m), the all-round views are tremendous, especially looking northwards to the North Sea where, on clear days, the estuary of the River Tees and the Durham coast can be seen on the horizon.

2. **At the beacon, where the lane bends left, do not bear right in the Lealholm direction but turn right along a vehicle track which descends gently across the open moorland to a lane. Turn right and after ¼ mile (400m), turn left, at a public footpath sign, down to a gate. Go through, head downhill along an enclosed track and at the bottom where the track curves left, turn right over a ladder stile and descend steps to a narrow lane.**

3. **Turn right and after just over ½ mile (800m) where the lane bends sharply to the left, keep ahead along a track towards farm**

Combination of woodland and moorland near Danby

buildings. Pass between the buildings, going through two gates, and continue along an enclosed path to another gate. Go through, continue downhill along an enclosed path and where it bends left down to a house, keep ahead over a stile and walk along the right edge of a field beside woodland. After passing between a tree and the end of a wall, bear left away from the edge and walk across the field, making for a gate and fingerpost. Go through the gate onto a road and turn right to return to the start.

Danby Beacon

Walk 11. Lealholm and the River Esk

Introduction

The only major valley of the North York Moors is that of the River Esk, a sparkling and unspoilt river for the whole of its length. This easy walk takes you through some of the glorious scenery of Upper Esk Dale around the village of Lealholm and provides you with some fine riverside walking and grand and extensive views over the valley and surrounding moors.

Distance	3 miles/4.8km
Start	Lealholm, car park, grid ref NZ764076
Parking	Free car park at Lealholm
Getting there by car	Lealholm is about 10 miles east of Whitby, from the A169 take the winding road through Esk Dale via Grosmont, Egton Bridge and Glaisdale
Public transport	There is a bus service (M&D Mini Coach 99) and a Northern Rail train service from Whitby but both are infrequent
Terrain	Field and riverside paths
Refreshments	Pub and café at Lealholm
Map	OS Explorer OL27

The Walk

For centuries Lealholm, situated where the valley of the Esk widens out, has been an important crossing point on the river. It is a particularly attractive spot, with a fine old bridge over the Esk, village green, stone cottages rising above the river and an appealing old church. The short, slim church tower that looks out of proportion with the rest of the building only adds to its appeal. The village is also an excellent walking centre, with enticing footpaths radiating from it in all directions.

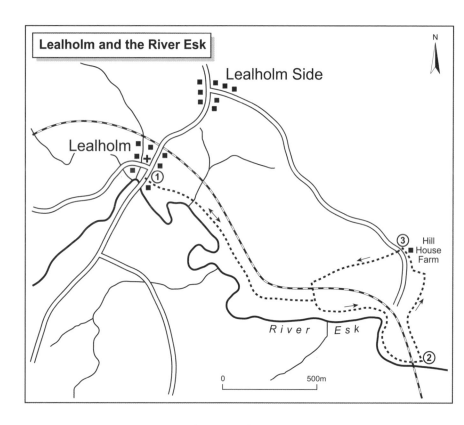

1. From the car park, turn left along the track, signposted to Glaisdale,
   which keeps above or beside the River Esk. After going through a
   gate, keep ahead towards a farm, turn right at a fingerpost and the
   track curves left and right and left again between farm buildings
   to a gate. Go through and continue beside the river, climbing above
   it and curving right to another gate. Go through, cross a footbridge
   over a beck and keep ahead to a track. Turn right and follow the
   Esk around a left bend. Do not cross the footbridge over the river
   but keep ahead towards the railway viaduct, climb a ladder stile
   and pass under the viaduct.

   The viaduct carries the Esk Valley railway line over the river. The
   railway, originally built from Whitby to Grosmont in 1835, was later
   extended in stages to link Whitby with Middlesbrough, a distance of

around 36 miles. It is considered to be one of the most attractive railway journeys in the whole of Britain.

2. Immediately turn left along a left field edge beside the embankment, heading up to a stile. Climb it and continue steadily uphill, by a wire fence on the left. On approaching farm buildings, go through a waymarked gate and head diagonally across a narrow field to a stile. Climb it, keep ahead gently uphill and turn left over a stile in the top left hand field corner. Continue by a hedge on the right and look out for a gap in the hedge where you turn right over a stile. Walk across a field to a fingerpost, climb a stile and turn left along a track. Go through a gate onto a narrow lane and keep ahead.

3. At a public bridleway sign, turn left down a track to a gate. Go through and as you continue along the top of a low ridge, there are superb views ahead over Esk Dale. Descend gently by the left edge of a small strip of woodland, keep to the left of a gate and continue

Lovely View over Esk Dale

Railway bridge over the River Esk

by a wire fence on the right, heading down to another gate. Go through, head down a track parallel to the railway line and turn left to go under a railway bridge. Continue through a farmyard and after going through a gate, turn right onto a track, at a public bridleway sign. Here you rejoin the outward route and retrace your steps to the start.

Walk 12. Rail Trail:
Goathland to Grosmont

Introduction

The combination of a leisurely and highly enjoyable ride on a steam train with a relaxing and attractive walk is an unforgettable experience, especially if blessed with fine weather. For the most part the Rail Trail follows the line of the original horse-drawn railway opened in 1836 and

Distance	4 miles/6.4km
Start	Goathland, railway station, grid ref NZ835014. Catch a North Yorkshire Moors Railway steam train from Grosmont and get off at the first stop at Goathland. For information on timetables phone 01751 472508
Finish	Grosmont railway station, grid ref NZ827053
Parking	Station car park at Grosmont
Getting there by car	Grosmont is about 9 miles to the east of Whitby, from the A169 take the road through Esk Dale signposted to Grosmont
Public transport	You can catch either Northern Rail or North Yorkshire Moors Railway trains from Whitby to Grosmont
Terrain	Easy and generally flat walking mainly through a wooded valley
Refreshments	Pubs and cafés at Goathland, pub and cafés at Grosmont, tea rooms at both stations, pub at Beck Hole
Map	OS Explorer OL27

later abandoned because it was unsuitable when the line was converted to steam locomotives. After a gentle descent along the incline between Goathland and Beck Hole – gentle for walkers if not for steam trains – the remainder of the route is through a mixture of woodland and more open country following the valley of the Murk Esk. Leave plenty of time to explore the many features of interest in the two villages at either end of the walk.

The Walk

The North Yorkshire Moors Railway operates steam trains through the heart of the national park, mainly between Pickering and Grosmont but recently some of the trains have been extended to Whitby. The original line was built by George Stephenson and opened in 1836 as a horse-drawn railway. After it was bought by George Hudson, the 'Railway King' in 1845, he began converting it into a steam railway. Essential improvements and adjustments were carried out but the major problem was the gradient of the incline between Goathland and Beck Hole which was too steep for the

Steam trains at Grosmont Station

Goathland station

locomotives. Therefore a new 4 mile stretch of line, the Deviation Line, was built in 1865 and this is the present route of the railway. Exactly one hundred years later the line was closed down but due to the work of amateur enthusiasts and volunteers, the line was saved and since its reopening in 1973 it has become a major tourist attraction. Another bonus is that the original 1836 line abandoned when the Deviation Line was opened, has been converted into an attractive footpath, the Goathland to Grosmont Rail Trail, the route taken by this walk.

1. **Leave the station at Goathland and walk up the hill into the village.**

    For details of Goathland see Walk 14.

    Take the first road on the right, signposted to Darnholm and Beck Hole, and just beyond the car park, turn left through a kissing gate, at a public footpath sign Grosmont Rail Trail. Head gently downhill to a kissing gate, cross a lane, go through a kissing gate opposite,

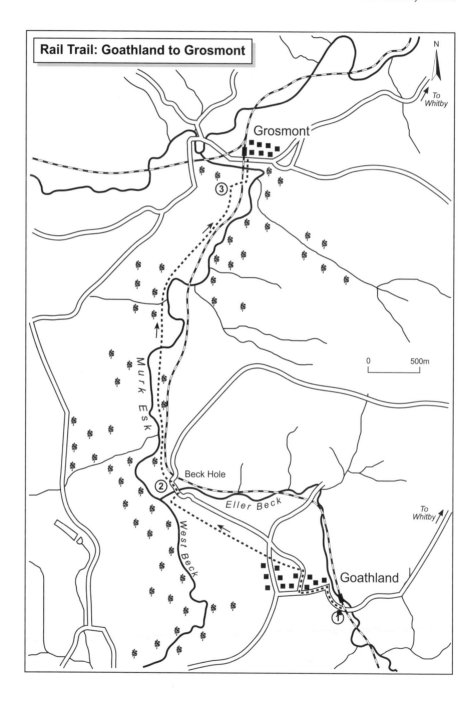

Rail Trail: Goathland to Grosmont

continue gently downhill through trees and go through another kissing gate soon after emerging from them. Keep ahead, passing Incline Cottage, built as a pair of railway cottages, and at a fingerpost, turn right in the Beck Hole direction, here making a brief diversion from the Rail Trail. Go through a gate, walk along a track, go through another gate onto a lane and turn left through the hamlet of Beck Hole.

Although comprising little more than a farm, a few cottages and pub, it is well worth making the diversion into the picturesque hamlet of Beck Hole even if you are not hungry or thirsty. The pub, the Birch Hall, is a fascinating old place comprising two bars separated by a sweet shop. In the smaller bar, one of the smallest in the country, the open fire creates a particularly cosy atmosphere on cold days.

Cross the bridge over Eller Beck and continue along the lane.

The Rail Track passes through beautiful woodland

2. Where the lane bends right at the start of an ascent, go through a gate, at a public footpath sign to Egton Bridge and Egton. Walk along an enclosed path and continue through woodland to a fingerpost where you rejoin the Rail Trail. Climb the stile ahead, continue through a lovely stretch of woodland, by the Murk Esk River on the left, climbing and descending steps to reach a footbridge. Keep ahead and on emerging from the trees, go through a gate and continue through more open country. After going through another gate and crossing a footbridge over the river, the route continues along a tree-lined path, going through several gates to reach the hamlet of Esk Valley, built in the 19th century to house workers from the local ironstone mines. The path now keeps beside the present railway line but look out for a Grosmont Rail Trail sign where you turn left through a kissing gate and turn right along an enclosed path parallel to the line. Head gently uphill, climb steps, go through a gate at the top and continue above the engine sheds on the edge of Grosmont, heading up to a gate. Ahead is a superb view over Grosmont and Esk Dale.

The superb view over Grosmont and Esk Dale near the end of the walk

3. **After going through the gate, turn right downhill along a tree-lined track to a gate. Go through, keep ahead and at a Rail Trail sign, turn left through a kissing gate and head down a broad track, passing to the left of Grosmont's 19th century church. At the bottom cross a footbridge over the River Esk, keep ahead to the road by Grosmont station and turn left to the car park.**

Grosmont is almost entirely a product of the railway and during the second half of the 19th century was something of a 'boom town'. As well as being an important junction where the Pickering to Grosmont line joined the Esk Valley line between Whitby and Middlesbrough, the railway led to the opening up of the local ironstone mines. Now it has reverted to being a quiet backwater once more although it would be quieter still but for the visitors attracted here by the North Yorkshire Moors Railway. Steam rail enthusiasts will enjoy pottering around the station and adjacent buildings, visiting the engine sheds and looking at all the railway memorabilia.

Walk 13. Falling Foss

Introduction

Although attractive and absorbing at any time of year and in all weathers, this delightful walk is ideal for a summer afternoon. Most of it is through the woodland that clothes both sides of the steep valley of May Beck and the highlight is the spectacular waterfall of Falling Foss at the approximate half-way point.

Distance	2½ miles/4km
Start	Forestry Commission North Riding Forest Park car park at May Beck, grid ref NZ893025
Parking	Free car park at May Beck
Getting there by car	May Beck is about 5 miles south of Whitby. From the A171 take the B1416 and turn off onto the lane signposted to May Beck
Public transport	None
Terrain	Undulating paths through woodland and by a beck
Refreshments	Falling Foss Tea Garden at Midge Hall beside the waterfall
Map	OS Explorer OL27

The Walk

1. From the car park turn right and almost immediately right again onto a stony track. After a few yards, turn left up a flight of steps and continue up to a gate. Go through and the path curves right and continues through woodland. Ignoring all stiles and side paths,

Falling Foss

keep ahead on the main path along the top left edge of the trees, eventually descending to a T-junction. Turn right downhill along a track and just in front of a bridge over May Beck, turn left down to Midge Hall and Falling Foss.

Situated in the middle of woodland at the hub of a network of public footpaths, it would be hard to find a more picturesque spot than this and a more relaxing setting in which to enjoy a refreshment break. Midge Hall was originally built as a gamekeepers' cottage in the late 18th century by the local landowner. At the beginning of the 20th century it became a tea garden, much frequented by ramblers, but subsequently fell into a state of dereliction. In recent years it has been restored and has now reopened as a popular tea garden once more. Next to it is the impressive waterfall of Falling Foss, where the water cascades through trees down to the beck.

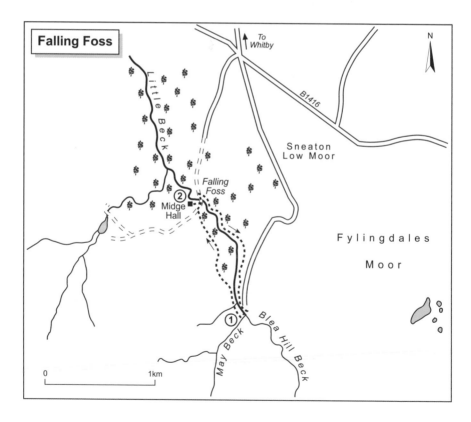

Wooded Valley of May Beck

2. Walk back up to the track, turn left over the bridge and the track curves uphill to Falling Foss car park. Turn right through the car park and at the far end, continue along a woodland track. Now comes a most attractive part of the route as you keep along this undulating track – it later narrows to a path – descending to cross a footbridge and continuing alongside May Beck. Head up, via steps in places, to a gate, go through and keep ahead. The path descends again for a final stretch beside the beck to a bridge. Turn right over it and right again to return to the car park.

Walk 14. Goathland and Mallyan Spout

Introduction

Although a short walk, it is full of interest, variety and fine views. The first part is a gradual descent along the track of a former railway, with the option of a brief diversion into the hamlet of Beck Hole. From here the route continues through, or sometimes above, the narrow and steep-sided gorge of West Beck to the dramatic waterfall of Mallyan Spout. After walking across the base of the fall, a steep climb via steps out of the gorge leads up to a lane which you follow back to Goathland.

Note that the short stretch of the path below Mallyan Spout is narrow, rocky and quite difficult to negotiate. Less agile or adventurous walkers, or those with children, who wish to avoid this can turn back and follow an easier path to Goathland after they have viewed the fall.

Distance	3½ miles/5.6km
Start	Goathland, car park at the north end of the village, grid ref NZ834014
Parking	Car park at Goathland
Getting there by car	Goathland lies on a loop road off the A169 9 miles to the south west of Whitby
Public transport	Yorkshire Coastliner bus 840 from Whitby
Terrain	Apart from an easy path at the beginning and a final stretch along a lane, most of the route is along a sometimes steep and rocky path through a gorge
Refreshments	Pubs ands cafés at Goathland, pub at Beck Hole
Map	OS Explorer OL27

Mallyan Spout

The Walk

In recent years Goathland has become well-known as the location of the village of Aidensfield in the television series 'Heartbeat' but its grand moorland setting, extensive network of public footpaths and station on the steam-hauled North Yorkshire Moors Railway has always made it a popular destination for walkers. It is a widely spaced village that stretches for over ¾ mile (1.2km) from the chunky Victorian church at the south end to the station at the north end. Sheep grazing on the spacious greens only emphasise its moorland location.

1. **Start by taking the road that runs alongside the car park (Beck Hole Road). Just before the road curves left, turn left through a kissing gate, at a public footpath sign Grosmont Rail Trail, and head gently downhill along a path to another kissing gate.**

   The first part of the walk between Goathland and Beck Hole descends the Beck Hole Incline, part of the original horse-drawn railway between

Sheep graze on the wide village greens at Goathland

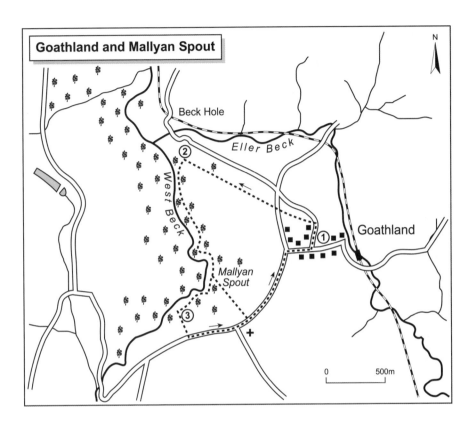

Pickering and Whitby built by George Stephenson in the 1830s. The 1:15 gradient was too steep for the horses and a pulley system was used by which the wagons coming down the incline hauled those that were coming up. When steam locomotives were later introduced, this method obviously became obsolete and a new route, the one currently used by the North Yorkshire Moors Railway, was cut. Nowadays the original line has been converted into the Rail Trail, an easy and attractive route for walkers and cyclists.

Go through the kissing gate, cross a road, go through a gate opposite and continue gently downhill along a tree-lined track. After the next kissing gate, keep ahead to Incline Cottage, originally a pair of railway cottages, to a footpath sign to the Mallyan. If you want to make a brief detour into the hamlet of Beck Hole, keep

Goathland is the setting for the village of Aidensfield in the
Heartbeat television series

ahead to the next footpath post and turn right along a track to
emerge onto a lane and turn left.

For details on Beck Hole see Walk 12.

2. **At the footpath sign to the Mallyan turn left. You now follow a path
    either through or above the narrow, wooded gorge of West Beck
    for the next 1¼ miles (2km), up and down flights of steps, across
    footbridges, sometimes along duckboards and through a series of
    kissing gates. Soon after passing a fingerpost, you see Mallyan
    Spout ahead.**

At 70 feet (213m) Mallyan Spout is the highest waterfall in the North
York Moors national park and is a popular venue for walkers in the
area. It is an impressive sight, perhaps seen at its best in winter or

early spring when the trees that line the side of the gorge are not in leaf.

As the short stretch of the path that passes across the base of the spout is rocky and quite difficult in places, some walkers might prefer an easier alternative. Simply retrace your steps to the fingerpost, turn right and follow a path which leads back to Goathland, rejoining the full walk on the lane at the south end of the village by the Mallyan Spout Hotel.

For the full walk, take care as you continue below the spout, beyond which you ascend and then descend more steps. Turn right to cross a footbridge over the beck and continue along the other bank to the next footbridge where you recross the beck.

3. After climbing a stile, bear left away from the beck and climb a long and quite tiring flight of steps cut into the side of the gorge. At the

Descending the incline between Goathland and Beck Hole

top of these steps, turn first left and then the path curves right and continues quite steeply up to emerge onto a lane. Turn left and follow the lane back into Goathland, passing the 19th century church and Mallyan Spout Hotel to return to the start.

Walk 15. The Roman Road on Wheeldale Moor

Introduction

A pleasant walk on a wooded path alongside Wheeldale Beck is followed by a gradual climb and then a descent along a quiet moorland lane. Then comes the highlight of the route: a walk of just under 1 mile beside one of the best preserved stretches of Roman road in the country across

Distance	4 miles/6.4km
Start	At the end of a lane signposted to Roman Road to the south west of Goathland, grid ref SE815989
Parking	Small parking area at the start
Getting there by car	From the south end of Goathland village (by the church and Mallyan Spout Hotel), take the lane signposted to Egton Bridge and Roman Road. After ½ mile, turn left, still in Roman Road direction, and the car park is about 1 mile along this lane by a Welcome to Goathland Estate information board and a sign forbidding unauthorised vehicles to go any further
Public transport	None
Terrain	Wooded path beside a beck, quiet lane, and moorland paths; the latter are rocky in places and may be muddy after wet weather
Refreshments	None en route but pubs and cafés 2 miles away in Goathland village
Map	OS Explorer OL27

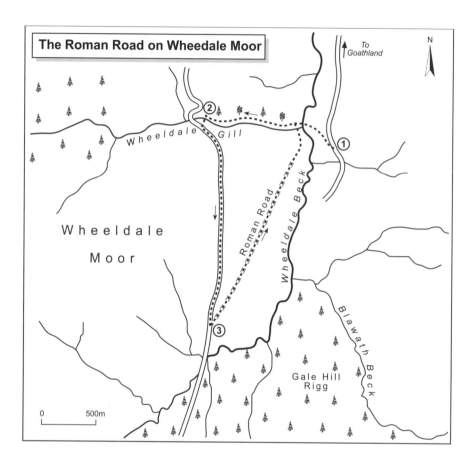

Wheeldale Moor, enjoying grand and extensive views in all directions. An easy descent into the valley leads you back to the start.

The Walk

1. **Start by turning right out of the car park, not back along the lane but along a parallel track, signposted to Roman Road, which descends to a gate. Go through, keep ahead to join a beck and shortly after going through the next gate, turn left, at another Roman Road footpath sign, to cross a footbridge over the beck. Turn right and right again to cross another footbridge over a wider beck (Wheeldale Beck), turn right on the other side and turn**

left over a stile. Walk across a field, keeping parallel to the beck, and climb a stile on the far side. Turn left, follow the path as it turns right at a yellow waymark and walk through trees beside Wheeldale Beck, a most attractive part of the route. Go through a gate, continue through conifers, go through another gate at the far end of the trees, keep ahead and turn left over a footbridge to a lane.

2. Turn left and keep along the lane for 1¼ miles (2km). At first it ascends, then flattens out and continues across the open moorland before dropping into a dip.

3. Before reaching the bottom of the dip, turn left over a stile, at a public footpath sign Roman Road, and walk along a path, indistinct at times, across Wheeldale Moor keeping parallel to the Roman road on the left.

Wheeldale Beck

The exposed section of Roman Road

This exposed stretch of the Roman Road, alternatively known as Wade's Causeway, runs for just under 1 mile (1.6km) across the open terrain of Wheeldale Moor. It is thought to have been built by the Romans to link their camp at Cawthorne to the south with the small fort at Lease Rigg to the north. As with all ancient routeways that are difficult to date precisely, some historians and archaeologists have cast doubts on the traditional interpretation, suggesting that it may predate the Roman period or even be later. Whatever its origins, it is undeniably atmospheric, makes a spectacular walk and is generally regarded as one of the finest stretches of Roman road anywhere in Britain.

Climb a ladder stile and keep ahead over increasingly uneven and rocky ground, heading gently downhill towards a gate. This is where the exposed stretch of the Roman road ends. After going through the gate, keep ahead by a wall on the right down to a stile. Climb it, bear left across grass to join a track and head downhill.

Where the track bends right, continue down to a stile, climb it and keep ahead by Wheeldale Beck again. Ignore the first footbridge on the left but cross the second one. Here you rejoin the outward route and retrace your steps to the start.

Walk 16. Whisper Dales and Broxa Forest

Introduction

If you want to get away from crowds and enjoy a quiet walk in attractive, secluded, wooded countryside then this is the one for you. A track leads gently downhill through the conifers of Broxa Forest into Whisper Dales and you continue by a sparkling beck through Low Dales. The second half of the route is a gentle ascent through another quiet dale, re-entering the forest to return to the start.

Distance	5 miles/8km
Start	Forestry Commission North Riding Forest Park car park at Reasty Bank, grid ref SE965945
Parking	Free car park at Reasty Bank
Getting there by car	Reasty Bank is about 6 miles north west of Scarborough. Take the A171 towards Whitby, turn left at a sign for Suffield, National Park and Hackness, follow signs for Hackness and at a T-junction on the edge of Suffield turn right in the Harwood Dale direction. The car park is about 3 miles along this road and extends over both sides of the road
Public transport	None
Terrain	Tracks, paths and a narrow lane through forest and dales
Refreshments	None
Map	OS Explorer OL27

The Walk

Right from the start there is a superb view looking northwards from the car park over Harwood Dale and eastwards towards the coast. Large swathes of the North York Moors National Park are covered by Forestry Commission conifer plantations and Broxa Forest is one of these. It makes an excellent venue for walking and cycling activities and mainly comprises pine and other conifers but there are also areas of semi-natural woodland and open heathland. Whisper Dales is one of a number of narrow and tranquil valleys that thread their way through it.

1. **At a public bridleway sign in the car park on the south side of the road, take the broad track that heads into the forest. The track heads gently downhill and after bearing left, continues more steeply down and emerges from the trees into Whisper Dales. Go through a gate in the valley bottom and keep ahead along the bottom left edge of a series of fields by Whisperdales Beck. After crossing the beck, continue along an enclosed track and where the**

The view from the start looking over Harwood Dale

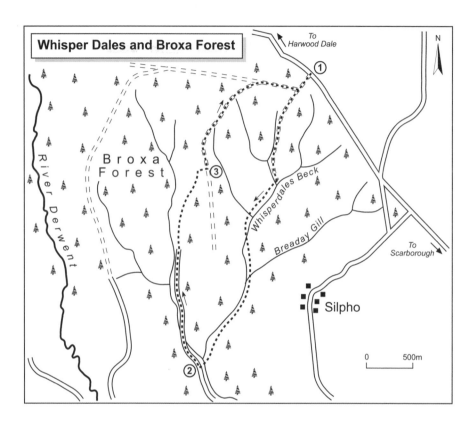

track curves left on entering a field, keep ahead across grass to a gate on the far side. Go through, keep ahead through the valley – the beck is now over to the right – and go through two more gates to reach Lowdales Farm. Cross two footbridges in quick succession, turn right to cross two more and turn right along a lane.

2. Follow this narrow lane gently uphill – it later becomes a rough track – pass to the left of a farm, and keep ahead to reach a pair of gates. Go through the right hand gate – there is a public bridleway sign – and head uphill along an enclosed path to re-enter the conifers of Broxa Forest. Cross a track and continue steadily uphill, emerging into a more open area of felled trees where the path forks. Take the right hand path which bends right to a T-junction where there is a blue-waymarked post.

Broxa Forest

3. Turn left along a broad clear track which re-enters woodland and look out for another broad, well-surfaced track where you turn right. The track curves first left and then right and continues to a T-junction. Turn left, here rejoining the outward route, and retrace your steps to the start.

Walk 17. Hole of Horcum

Introduction

This walk around part of the rim and across the bottom of the vast natural amphitheatre of the Hole of Horcum provides you with a series of extensive and dramatic views, both over the 'hole' itself and across the seemingly endless moors. From the eastern rim you descend into the bottom and continue across it, much of the time beside Levisham Beck. An easy climb brings you up to the western rim and the finale is a glorious 2 mile (3.2km) walk along a clear moorland track from which there are grand views in all directions across an open and largely empty landscape.

Distance	5 miles/8km
Start	Hole of Horcum, car park beside A619, grid ref SE853937
Parking	Free car park at Hole of Horcum
Getting there by car	Hole of Horcum is on the A169 12 miles south of Whitby
Public transport	Yorkshire Coastliner bus 840 from Whitby
Terrain	Paths and tracks across moorland and along valley bottom, gentle climbing, some muddy stretches likely
Refreshments	None
Map	OS Explorer OL27

The Walk

1. Cross the road from the car park, go down some steps and turn right onto a path that runs along the eastern rim of the 'hole' parallel to the A169.

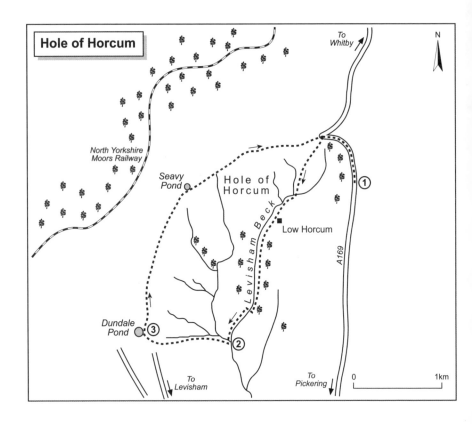

Right from the start the views over the Hole of Horcum are superb. According to legend, this huge natural amphitheatre was created by a giant who scooped it out with his hand but the more likely, if also the less exciting explanation is that it was formed as a result of erosion caused by torrents of glacial meltwater at the end of the Ice Age. Whichever you prefer, it is one of the scenic highlights of the North York Moors national park.

The path follows the curve of the rim to the left and where the road turns sharply to the right, bear left onto a narrower path that heads downhill to a stile. Climb it, continue down between heather to the bottom and keep ahead to a stile and gate. Immediately beyond

these the path forks. Take the right hand path, which just after passing the ruined Low Horcum Farm, curves first left and then right. At the next fork, take the right hand path which continues across the bottom of the valley and just before reaching a waymarked gate, there is another fork. Again take the right hand lower path which continues by the right edge of sloping woodland to a gate. Go through, keep ahead between trees – there are boardwalks in places – and continue along this path beside Levisham Beck as far as a footbridge over the beck. Cross it and just after fording a smaller beck, you reach a fingerpost.

2. Turn right, in the Dundale Road direction, along a path which climbs steadily uphill above a beck on the right. At a fork, take the right hand path which continues gently up to a fingerpost.

3. Turn right, in the Saltersgate direction, along a broad path which follows the western rim of the Hole of Horcum across the top of

The Hole of Horcum looks impressive at any time of the year

The Great natural amphitheatre of the Hole of Horcum

the moorland, curving gradually right all the time. After 2 miles (3.2km) you reach a stile/gate. Climb or go through, shortly rejoining the outward route, and retrace your steps to the start.

Walk 18. Lockton, Newton Dale and Levisham

Introduction

The twin moorland villages of Lockton and Levisham are scarcely more than ½ mile (800m) apart but are separated by a deep wooded ravine. The walk starts off by descending into that ravine and then follows the valley of Levisham Beck, crossing the line of the North Yorkshire Moors Railway where two valleys meet. It then heads back along the side of Newton Dale, climbing gently through woodland and across fields before plunging down to recross the railway line at Levisham station. Then comes a steep climb into Levisham village, an equally steep descent into the ravine that divides it from Lockton and a final ascent back to the start. This is a most memorable walk, worth saving for a fine day, which combines two attractive villages with beautiful woodland walking and superb moorland views.

Distance	6½ miles/10.5km
Start	Lockton, by the church, grid ref SE844900
Parking	Roadside parking at Lockton
Getting there by car	Lockton lies just off the A169 about 15 miles south of Whitby
Public transport	Yorkshire Coastliner bus 840 from Whitby to the end of Lockton Lane, from there it is just over ¼ mile (400m) to the village centre
Terrain	Mostly wooded valleys and hillsides, two fairly steep climbs
Refreshments	Tea room at Lockton, pub at Levisham
Map	OS Explorer OL27

Lockton Church

The Walk

Despite being only ¼ mile (400m) from the main Pickering to Whitby road, the village of Lockton has a definite air of remoteness. Its stone cottages and small medieval church appear to match their moorland surroundings perfectly.

1. **With the church on your right, walk through the village and at a junction keep ahead along the lane signposted as a 'No Through Road'. Where the lane ends, go up steps to the right of a gatepost and continue along an enclosed path. Follow the path around a right bend and descend steps to a junction of paths at the top edge of steeply sloping woodland. Head downhill through the trees to emerge onto a lane and immediately turn left along a track.**

    Soon you see the tower of a ruined church on the right. This is St Mary's, the former parish church of Levisham which fell into ruin after being abandoned and replaced by a new church more conveniently located in the village centre.

Keep along this track for the next 1¼ miles (2km), going through a succession of gates, and eventually the track curves right to a junction.

2. Keep ahead through a gate, continue beside a beck, pass between farm buildings and cross the track of the North Yorkshire Moors Railway. Bear right to cross a footbridge, continue along a wooded track and where this track starts to ascend, look out for a public footpath sign where you bear right along a path. The next part of the route takes you through the lovely, thickly-wooded and steep-sided Newton Dale. At first the path continues through trees but

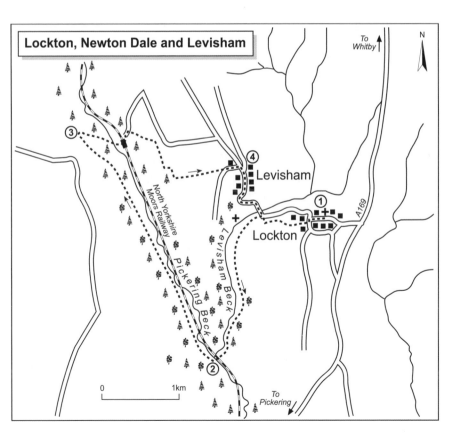

later you cross fields, going through another succession of gates and heading gently uphill all the time. After 2 miles (3.2km) near the top edge of the valley, look out for where another path comes in from the left and keep ahead to a waymarked gate.

3. Do not go through it but turn sharp right and head downhill across the rough, uneven field, looking for a gap in the bushes ahead. Go through the gap, head down to the bottom left hand corner of the field and continue steeply down a clearer path through gorse and trees towards Levisham station. Cross a footbridge over a beck and keep ahead to the station buildings.

Over many years volunteers have worked hard to restore Levisham station to what a small country station would have looked like in the years before the outbreak of the First World War. One of the buildings is used as a studio by the North Yorkshire Moors Railway's own artist and is frequently open. Given its location, surrounded by an extensive

The remote Levisham station

Looking down on Newton Dale

network of public footpaths and adjacent to some outstanding scenery, it is not surprising that the station is a popular destination for walkers on fine weekends and bank holidays.

After recrossing the line, head uphill along a lane and at a public footpath sign to Levisham, turn right, cross a footbridge and go through a gate. Ascend steeply through trees to a gate at the top edge of the woodland, go through and continue uphill by the left edge of a field, curving right to another gate. After going through that one, keep ahead to a fork and take the left hand uphill grassy path. From here there are superb views over Newton Dale. The path later curves left between gorse bushes, then curves right and continues more steeply uphill to a stile. Climb it, turn left, keep along the left edge of two fields to emerge onto a narrow lane and follow it into the village of Levisham.

Levisham comprises one main street, flanked by wide greens with the cottages set well back from the road. The pub is at the top and nearby is a small Victorian church, the successor of the ruined one seen soon after the start of the walk. Unlike Lockton, Levisham really is remote: linked to Lockton and the A165 only by a narrow, steep, twisting lane and over 1 mile (1.6km) away from and over 300 feet (91m) above its station that is only regularly in use during the summer months.

4. **Turn right by the Horseshoe Inn and walk down the village street. Continue steeply downhill along a twisting lane through woodland and where the lane bears left soon after starting to ascend, keep ahead up steps at a public footpath sign. Here you rejoin the outward route and retrace your steps up through the trees back to Lockton.**

One of the lovely, steep-sided, wooded valleys around Lockton and Levisham

Walk 19. Forge Valley Woods and Ayton Castle

Introduction

After an opening stretch along the road into East Ayton, you cross the River Derwent into West Ayton for the start of a beautiful walk along the west bank of the river through the narrow, steep-sided and thickly-

Distance	4 miles/6.4km
Start	Forge Valley Woods National Nature Reserve car park at Seavegate Gill, grid ref SE989856
Parking	Forge Valley Woods (free)
Getting there by car	Forge Valley is about 4 miles west of Scarborough. Take the A170 to East Ayton and turn right along the road signposted to Forge Valley and Hackness; the car park at Seavegate Gill is ½ mile north of the village, the first of a series of parking areas on this road
Public transport	None to the starting point but Scarborough and District bus 128 from Scarborough stops at West Ayton where you could join the route
Terrain	Woodland walking either beside the river or high up above the valley; two climbs, one steep and the other moderate, on the second half of the walk
Refreshments	Pubs at East and West Ayton
Map	OS Explorer OL27

wooded Forge Valley. After recrossing the river to the east bank, the return is mostly along wooded paths high up above the valley. The Forge Valley is a popular walking area and the paths can get churned up after wet weather but fortunately much of the riverside path is on well-constructed duckboards.

The Walk

1. **Turn left out of the car park along the road above the River Derwent into East Ayton. At a T-junction turn right, cross the bridge over the river into West Ayton and immediately turn right along Mill Lane. Follow the lane around a left bend to a T-junction and turn right gently uphill.**

2. **At a public footpath sign to Forge Valley, turn right along a tarmac track, go through a kissing gate and keep ahead across a field, passing to the right of the ruins of Ayton Castle.**

The Rive Derwent flows through the wooded Forge Valley

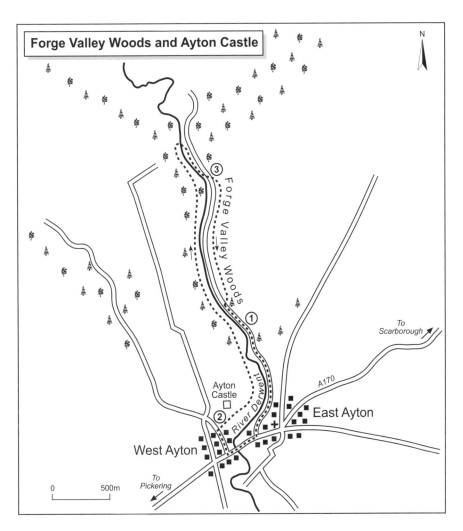

Despite its name, Ayton Castle was more of a fortified medieval manor house than a castle and was the home of the local Ayton family. Later owners abandoned it and it fell into ruin. All that is left standing is the three-storied 14th century tower house, an impressive structure.

Continue across the field and after going through a gate you enter the Forge Valley Woods National Nature Reserve.

Accessible footpaths and the beauty of the woodlands that clothe its steep sides ensure that the Forge Valley gets a steady stream of visitors from Scarborough and the surrounding area. It is a particular popular family venue for walks and picnics. The valley gets its name from a former forge in the area and there are also several disused quarries.

Descend gently, keep along the left edge of riverside meadows and after the next gate, the route continues on duckboards beside the River Derwent, a most attractive part of the route. After nearly 1 mile (1.6km), turn right over the first footbridge, turn right again on the other side and pass through a car park. At a footpath sign, go through a fence gap and continue beside the river. Turn left up steps, turn right to walk beside the wall bordering the road and turn left through a fence gap onto the road.

Ruins of Ayton Castle

Riverside path through the beautiful Forge Valley Woods

3. Cross over to a public footpath sign and take the right hand one of two paths ahead which climbs steeply through the dense woodland via a long flight of steps. Continue along the side of the valley high up above the road and river and the path later descends to a T-junction just above the road. Turn left uphill again and after bending right you reach a fork. Take the right hand lower path and follow it to an abandoned quarry. After passing through the quarry descend to a T-junction and turn right downhill along a track, passing through a car park onto the road. Turn left for the short distance back to the start.

Walk 20. Gristhorpe and Muston

Introduction

This walk is on the northern edge of the gentle, rolling, chalk country of the Yorkshire Wolds, a contrast with the other routes in this book which are predominantly coastal or moorland walks. From Gristhorpe the route leads along a quiet lane and field paths to a drainage channel which is then followed into Muston. Easy to follow hedge-lined tracks and paths lead back to the start. For most of the route there are wide views over the surrounding countryside.

Distance	4½ miles/7.2km
Start	Gristhorpe, by the Bull Inn, grid ref TA087819
Parking	Roadside parking at Gristhorpe
Getting there by car	Gristhorpe is just off the A165 2 miles from Filey and 6 miles south of Scarborough
Public transport	East Yorkshire bus 121 from Filey and Scarborough
Terrain	Flat field paths and tracks
Refreshments	Pub at Gristhorpe, pub at Muston
Map	OS Explorer 301

The Walk

The unassuming village of Gristhorpe lies between the sea and the edge of the Yorkshire Wolds and has a main street lined by attractive old cottages. In 1834 the remains of a prehistoric man were found in an oak coffin on the coast near here. Known as 'Gristhorpe Man', he is thought to be over 4000 years old and can be seen in the Rotunda Museum at Scarborough.

Attractive cottage line the village street at Gristhorpe

1. With the pub to your right, walk along the village street and beyond the last of the houses, follow the lane around a left bend and continue over a level crossing. The lane later becomes a tarmac track – though there is no obvious difference – and you keep along it to a farm. Where the track bends left, turn right along the right edge of farm buildings, follow the path to the left and continue along a fence-lined track to reach a drainage channel (Main Drain).

2. Turn left and walk beside it to a gate. Go through, keep ahead and in the field corner go through a kissing gate and continue along the right edge of the next two fields. In the corner of the last field, turn right through a kissing gate, walk across a field, crossing a concrete footbridge over a drain, and make for the next kissing gate. After going through it, follow the path around a left bend, go through a gate, continue along a tree-lined track and go through another kissing gate onto the main road in Muston. Turn left and follow the winding road through the village.

Muston is another pleasant village on the edge of the wolds. Its most picturesque spot is at the eastern end where the small Victorian

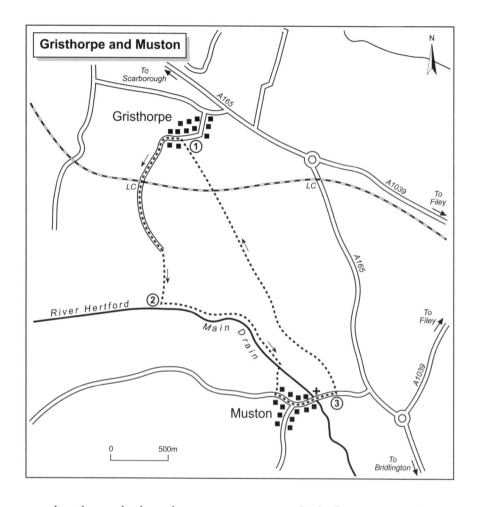

church overlooks a large green across which flows a meandering
stream crossed by several bridges.

3. **Just after a sharp left bend, bear left along King Street beside a
   triangular green and at a 'No Through Road' sign, turn left along
   Carr Lane. The lane later becomes a rough enclosed track which
   you follow to a fork. Take the right hand track and at a pair of
   gates, go through the left hand one and keep along an enclosed
   track. Later the route continues first along right field edges and
   later between fields to a stile. Climb it, cross a plank footbridge**

Looking across to the Victorian church from the village green at Muston

over a drain and walk along the left edge of two fields. In the corner of the second field, climb a stile and bear right to climb another one. Cross an iron footbridge over a drain, walk along the right edge of a field and carefully cross a railway line. Initially keep along the right edge of the next field but gradually bear left away from it making for a kissing gate. Go through and continue along a track by the right field edge, following the track as it bears left to a kissing gate. Go through, keep ahead by farm buildings and go through a gate onto the village street in Gristhorpe. Turn right to the starting point by the Bull Inn.

More books from Sigma Press

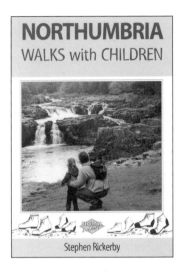

Northumbria Walks with Children
Stephen Rickerby

Over 20 walks are included covering the North East from the Tees to the Tweed. There are questions (with answers!) and checklists to both challenge and interest the children, as well as practical information for parents. All walks are less than 5 miles long, exploring the great variety of scenery and heritage of Northumbria.

'This is a splendid collection that will excite and stimulate youngsters.'
– Sunderland Echo

£7.95

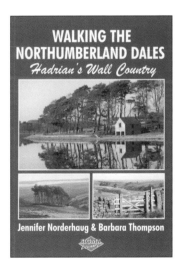

Walking The Northumberland Dales
Hadrian's Wall Country
Barbara Thompson

Explore the landscapes of North and South Tynedale, Allendale, Hexhamshire, Blanchland and Hadrian's Wall. The walks are packed with interest on the history, industrial archeology and the area's traditions, and culture.

£8.95

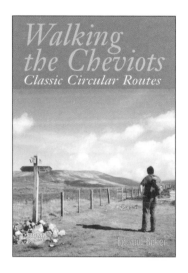

Walking the Cheviots
Classic Circular Routes
Edward Baker

The walks in this book provide an excellent introduction to this lonely, wild countryside — a true wilderness area. Everyone is catered for — from weekend family groups to the experienced hill walker. Each route is full of interest, with details of the natural history, geology and archaeology of the area.

£9.95

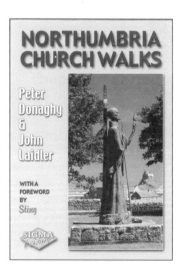

Northumbria Church Walks
Peter Donaghy & John Laidler
With a Foreword by Sting

30 circular walks, from 4 to 12 miles with alternative shorter options, combined with over 40 churches open to visitors with fine examples of stained glass, ancient crosses, medieval fonts, carvings and sculptures.

£8.95

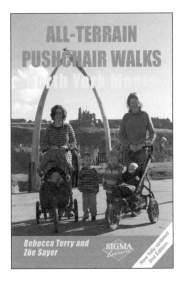

All-Terrain Pushchair Walks
The North York Moors
Zoë Sayer and Rebecca Terry

Explore the North York Moors — the perfect place to both keep fit and introduce your children to the delights of the outdoors. This fully revised and updated 2nd edition includes gradings and at-a-glance symbols to make walk choice easy and allow you to plan ahead. There are 30 walks spread across the entire national park from riverside walks and coastal strolls to rambles through the heather moors.

£8.99

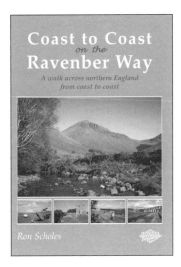

Coast to Coast
On the Ravenber Way
Ron Scholes

The walk described in the book follows existing rights of way in the form of footpaths, bridleways and tracks, making this cross-country route a challenging long-distance journey. The walk commences at Ravenglass, it passes Lakeland's finest array of high peaks, climbs over the high Pennines, traverses the northern moors and ends at Berwick-upon-Tweed.

£8.99

Available November 2010

All-Terrain Pushchair Walks: Yorkshire Dales
Rebecca Terry

Find out the best of what the Yorkshire Dales has to offer with these 30 tried and tested all-terrain pushchair walks through open moorland and country estates, and alongside the beautiful and dramatic rivers for which this National Park is renowned. The walks are all accurately graded and have at-a-glance symbols making choosing easier.

£7.95

Ghost Walks around York
Over 50 of York's haunted locations
David Shaw

For over 20 years David Shaw has been a regular visitor to the beautiful and historic city of York and during his pleasant stays gradually became aware of the enormous wealth of reported ghost sightings in the area. The walks in this illustrated book include descriptions of hauntings in 60 locations.

£7.99

Available October 2010

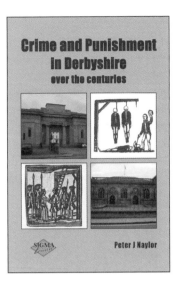

Derbyshire Crime
Over the centuries
Peter J Naylor

Crime fascinates us all, particularly murders, and the bloodier they are the better they are received. It would appear that the Peak District was a lawless place until more recent times. This book is a thorough mix of most of the types of crimes committed in Derbyshire over the centuries. Each chapter is dedicated to a different type of crime and the punishments handed out.

£8.99

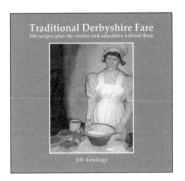

Traditional Derbyshire Fare
300 recipes plus the stories and anecdotes behind them
Jill Armitage

Some Derbyshire dishes, like the Bakewell Pudding, are well known; many more, including some of the most delectable, are little known outside the places whose name they bear. The recipes are individual, easy, economical, readily available, and have a strong regional accent. This is Derbyshire food at its best.

£12.99

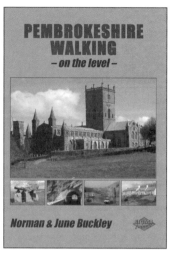

Pembrokeshire Walking
on the level
Norman and June Buckley

Discover both the breath-taking splendour of the Pembrokeshire coast and its diverse inland landscape. The 25 comparatively short, easy walks in this book include clear route directions, map and a brief description of features encountered along the way as well as recommendations for refreshment.

£8.99

Holiday Walks in North Wales
Brian Conduit

20 walks ranging from 2 to 6 miles in length, all within the capabilities of most people, varying in difficulty and the nature of the terrain. The scenery is varied and magnificent and the walks vary from easy and flat riverside strolls to more challenging walks in the Snowdonia National Park or on the slopes of the Clwydian hills.

£8.99

All of our books are available through booksellers.
For a free catalogue, please contact:

Sigma Leisure, Stobart House, Pontyclerc
Penybanc Road, Ammanford SA18 3HP

Tel: 01269 593100 Fax: 01269 596116

info@sigmapress.co.uk   www.sigmapress.co.uk